The Lang
Dreams & Visions

CAROL ANN HENLEY

CAROL ANN HENLEY

Scripture taken from the New King James Version®, Copyright ® 1982 by Thomas Nelson. Used with permission. All rights reserved.

First print edition, 2019

ISBN: 1-7906-5806-3
ISBN-13: 9781790658060

ENDORSEMENTS

It is with great pleasure and honour that I recommend the ministry of Carol Ann Henley. If you are looking to better understand how God communicates with us, this book offers a portal entry to a functional world of understanding the language of God. Carol Ann examines the scriptures with consistency as building blocks to grasp, confirm, and affirm the significance of dreams and visions. Her explanation shows the veracity of how God speaks in these ways. When we understand and interpret these messages, we can live fully in His purpose. I applaud the author for this helpful resource.

~ *Danyele Bloom Holtner, Aglow International Canada*

We met Carol Ann after a Global Gathering of spiritual fathers and mothers in Munich 2015, and afterwards she was ministering in our Church in Hof/Bavaria. Her interest in dreams was exciting for us, and we were so pleased when she offered to another couple and us to teach us online on dreams. This teaching enlarged our understanding how God is speaking to us through dreams. We typically thought of dreams to be a place of our soul to deal with emotions and experiences of the daytime. Now we saw how important they are in the whole Bible, and we started to look at our dreams as one way that God is actually talking with us even if He uses a symbolic language. But who are we to tell God which method He would have to use to communicate with us? We repented. Now we've got this course as a book, and it is so helpful to find the meaning of colours in dreams or even limbs for instance.

We are excited to read that listening to God's voice is not only a matter of paying attention to your dreams but also reading your Bible and praying especially by using the gift of tongues for hours. This book will become a special blessing for all who want to understand God's voice and will put into practice what is recommended and explained by this woman of God. It's a practical book for practical use.

~ *Rita and Herbert Lang, Evangelical Lutheran Pastors, Hof/Bavaria, Germany*

Whether the topic of dreams is new to you, or if you have studied it in the past, you will find Carol Ann Henley's book a refreshing look at this significant topic.

The Language of God is a combination of scriptural and historical facts, as well as practical instruction for those desiring to interpret dreams. This book will impact your life, as you come to know the language God uses, to speak to you.

~ Bonnie & Roger Rutter, Kingston, Ontario

I have known Carol Ann for over thirty years. Many times she has spoken into my life with scripture, and through dreams and visions, bringing me comfort, hope and encouragement when I needed it most.

I value her wisdom and insight as she challenges me to pray and go deeper in my relationship with God.

~ Kathie May, Manitoba, Canada

Carol Ann is an amazing woman of God who carries a Joesph anointing. Her teaching methods are easily comprehended and can be applied to any dream.

Carol Ann's insight into interpretation has helped me to discover new ways of unravelling my dreams.

I strongly recommend this book to anyone wanting a greater revelation to unlock what God is saying in their dreams.

~ Shell Rogers, Saskatchewan, Canada

Carol Ann has given the Body of Christ a valuable tool in order to help make hearing from God fun and easy!

The Language of God: Dreams and Visions is full of scripture references concerning dreams and dreamers, coupled with many real life examples and insightful symbolic meanings. This book is sure to bring back an assurance that God really wants to speak to His children through dreams!

I have known Carol Ann for over 25 years. As far back as I can remember, she has always been the person people went to in order to make sense of their dreams. I have also received insight from her concerning some of my own dreams. She serves the Body of Christ using her gifts with absolute humility and love. Her section on prayer has lit a fire in me!

I will be putting a pen and paper on my night table from now on, along with this book!

~ Gwen Mercer, Children's Church Director, Kelowna Harvest Fellowship, Kelowna, BC

Carol Ann has influenced my life in the area of dream interpretation for many years, which has helped me to navigate through some specific areas of my life. Because of her influence in this area it has brought encouragement and perspective when I have needed confirmation of what God was saying to me in my dreams. She brings sound teaching along with many personal examples of dream interpretation. This book is sure to help readers improve their own journey of understanding dreams from a biblical view.

~ Joan Bolton, Edmonton, Alberta

God has surely given Carol Ann a special gift. It will inspire you and encourage a deeper connection with our Father, Jesus and Holy Spirit. This book is a book of incredible wealth.

~ Fiona Ng, Toronto, Ontario

I have had the pleasure of knowing Carol Ann for more than thirty years and thus have had the privilege of sitting under her teaching and participating in her workshops. Carol Ann has interpreted many dreams my husband and I have had over the years with great accuracy. She is a gifted teacher who presents her material in an interesting and understandable format using many practical examples, which is reflected in this book. This book is a must read for anyone desiring to know more about understanding dreams and visions and how to interpret them.

~ Mary Murdoch, Sudbury, Ontario

CAROL ANN HENLEY

DEDICATION

This book about the language of God is dedicated to Him whose heart of love has been shared with me in dreams. His love has satisfied me.

FOREWORD

Dreams and visions are forms of communication found throughout the Bible. The Lord has spoken in the language of dreams and visions for millennia. The understanding and interpretation of the messages came through angels, men and women of God.

In recent times, we as the receivers of the messages often lack understanding to discern and decipher the meanings. Our inadequacy in understanding dreams and visions has left us at a disadvantage in what God is saying. Frequently people have ultimately not gotten the message.

Today, there is a growing desire in the Body of Christ to acquire the training and mentoring in the interpretation of dreams and visions. You have in your hands a straightforward and easy-to-use guide in this process. *The Language of God: Dreams and Visions* grew through Carol Ann's almost forty years experience learning the language of God.

Carol Ann has been a trusted friend for twenty years. She is a team player and prays through the dreams and visions she receives. She prays both for the meaning of each message and for God's purposes through them. She is a wife, mom and grandmother. She understands and walks in the biblical protocols needed for successful life and ministry. Carol Ann's maturity radiates from her abilities and capacity to function with others in the process of mutual submission and discernment of dream language.

On numerous occasions, I've enjoyed walking through the dynamic prophetic interpretation process with Carol Ann. She's had dreams releasing a 'word of the Lord' pertaining to our ministry, for our province and regarding the nations. In my experience it is not only her dream life that is powerful, it is a deep spiritually based confidence flowing through Carol Ann. Her biblical study and understanding allows the Lord to guide her in discernment, clarity and accuracy. In a variety of settings, I've seen her mentor and release quality insight concerning the fullness of God's message to individuals and groups.

It is in the light of this life of grace that I commend this book to you. Enjoy personal and spiritual growth as you study and ponder the pages of this book.

Thank you, Carol Ann, for your commitment to steward the gift Father set within you as a child. Your faithfulness has caused the Lord to increase the impact of your gift many times over.

~ Michael D. Pierce, Christ For Your City, August 2018

INTRODUCTION

From the time I was a child growing up, spending summers with my grandparents, I was taught about God. I was taught Bible stories about Jesus and how He loved the children and also taught to honour God in my life. My family, especially my mother and my grandfather, modelled this lifestyle to me. I loved these stories as a child and I loved hearing and seeing my family talking about their faith in God. As a child, I was a dreamer. I had vivid dreams but never understood them.

Later, when I was a young wife and mother, our little family moved away from home where my husband took on a more responsible role with the organization he worked for. Because he was very busy with his new job, I found that I was lonely and missed my family back home.

Eventually, I came into contact with Christian believers who encouraged me to give my life over to God. When I did my life changed completely. From the first day, I began to read the stories in the Bible and talk to God like He was a part of my life. I began to see how God talked to people in dreams and visions. However. I began having more dreams that I didn't understand. I was very curious and tried to get as much information as I could about dreams.

Years later, I heard about a course that was being offered by an international ministry that taught on hearing the voice of God and understanding how He communicated. I took the three modules offered. I have shared what I have learned with my children and grandchildren, and with many other believers.

One of the original teachers moved to Canada and came to our region to teach the same principles. He ultimately released me to teach this material.

Now, 40 years after praying that prayer of personal commitment and nearly 10 years after beginning to teach on understanding how God speaks to us, I have felt that it's important for me to write these things down. Many have also asked me for a resource they can use. So, it's with this in mind that I have set out to capture the essentials of understanding dreams and visions.

CAROL ANN HENLEY

CONTENTS

CAROL ANN HENLEY

1 RESTORING A LOST LANGUAGE

Language is the key to personal relationships. It's possible to meet someone without speaking their language but it's rare to have relationship without a common language. I live in a community where it's normal for people to speak two languages. I have observed first-hand someone expressing themselves in their second language to a unilingual speaking person using words that had a negative connotation in the second language but the person didn't realize that and a misunderstanding was the result. From the misunderstanding, a breach formed in the relationship and this gap widened until there was no longer a working relationship.

Marriage counsellors always say that two-way communication is critical in a marriage relationship. Without two-way communication there is no true intimacy, no growth in the relationship.

Language is also a key to a thriving culture. Canada is a multicultural nation. It has two official languages, English and French, and cultures and languages of most of the nations of the world. Each group seeks to maintain their culture by teaching their language to their children, hoping that their culture will continue from generation to generation.

For instance, in the province of Nova Scotia, the current residents include descendants of Scotland. They made an effort to maintain the Gaelic language. They teach the language to children hoping to revive interest in Gaelic to a people who had been assimilated to a different culture. Their efforts have been so effective that some have been invited to go to Scotland to teach the language since their maintenance of Gaelic surpassed that of their original homeland.

The language of dreams and visions was once a language well understood in the ancient Hebraic culture. Unfortunately, it's been largely lost and almost unknown to those of us raised in the western culture. However, there is a new interest in this language and a desire to understand it, in that it is a key factor in our relationship with God.

2 DREAMS AND VISIONS: THEIR IMPORTANCE IN HISTORY

God is like a Dad speaking to his kids. He is communicating, but are we listening? Do we understand the message?

There are many references for the use of dreams, visions, riddles and parables in the Bible. God will sometimes give us a riddle to reflect on and figure out in a similar way that we might play scavenger hunt where we use clues to find items that we need in order to get to the next level of the game. It's a way to engage us and teach us.

As is explained in the following scripture verses:

> *It is the glory of God to conceal a matter, but the glory of kings is to search out a matter (Proverbs 25:2).*

> *For God may speak in one way, or in another, yet man does not perceive it. In a dream, in a vision of the night, when deep sleep falls upon men, while slumbering on their beds, then He opens the ears of men, and seals their instruction. In order to turn man from his deed, and conceal pride from man ... (Job 33:14-17).*

> *And when Saul inquired of the Lord, the Lord did not answer him, either by dreams or by Urim or by the prophets (1 Samuel 28:6).*

God uses dreams to speak. He uses dreams like parables and hides wisdom in them for us to search for understanding:

> *Son of man, pose a riddle, and speak a parable to the house of Israel (Ezekiel 17:2).*

Dreaming dreams and seeing visions is associated with the outpouring of the Holy Spirit:

> *And it shall come to pass afterward that I will pour out My Spirit on all flesh; your sons and your daughters shall prophesy, your old men shall dream dreams, your young men shall see visions (Joel 2:28).*

In Acts 2, Peter quoted this last reference as being fulfilled after the death and resurrection of Jesus and his ascension to the right hand of God. The Holy Spirit was given and the gift of the Holy Spirit was now available to all.

> *Then Peter said to them, "Repent, and let every one of you be baptized in the name of Jesus Christ for the remission of sins; and you shall receive the gift of the Holy Spirit. For the promise is to you and to your children, and to all who are afar off, as many as the Lord our God will call" (Acts 2:38-39).*

With the gift of the Holy Spirit, we can expect to see, hear of, and participate in prophesying, dreaming dreams, and seeing visions. It's a natural byproduct of the gift of, or infilling of, the Holy Spirit.

Dreams are one way for God to speak. And He wants us to figure out what He is saying in dreams.

DREAMS AND VISIONS IN HISTORY

God has used dreams and visions to speak to people in the Bible, in both the Old and New Testaments, as well as in modern history. Let's begin with some Old Testament examples.

Joseph and Pharaoh

Pharaoh, the leader of one of the largest nations of the era and the dominant economy of that time, had two dreams. He heard that Joseph had interpreted two dreams that came to pass three days later. Pharaoh decided to tell Joseph his dreams:

> *Then Pharaoh said to Joseph: "Behold, in my dream I stood on the bank of the river. Suddenly seven cows came up out of the river, fine looking and fat; and they fed in the meadow. Then behold, seven other cows came up after them, poor and very ugly and gaunt, such ugliness, as I have never seen in all the land of Egypt. And the gaunt and ugly cows ate up the first seven, the fat cows. When they had eaten them up, no one would have known that they had eaten them, for they were just as ugly as at the*

beginning. So I awoke. Also I saw in my dream, and suddenly seven heads came up on one stalk, full and good. Then behold, seven heads, withered, thin, and blighted by the east wind, sprang up after them. And the thin heads devoured the seven good heads. So I told this to the magicians, but there was no one who could explain it to me."

Then Joseph said to Pharaoh, "The dreams of Pharaoh are one; God has shown Pharaoh what He is about to do: The seven good cows are seven years, and the seven good heads are seven years; the dreams are one. And the seven thin and ugly cows, which came up after them, are seven years, and the seven empty heads blighted by the east wind are seven years of famine. This is the thing, which I have spoken to Pharaoh. God has shown Pharaoh what He is about to do. Indeed seven years of great plenty will come throughout all the land of Egypt; but after them seven years of famine will arise, and all the plenty will be forgotten in the land of Egypt; and the famine will deplete the land. So the plenty will not be known in the land because of the famine following, for it will be very severe. And the dream was repeated to Pharaoh twice because the thing is established by God, and God will shortly bring it to pass" (Genesis 41: 17-32).

Figure 1: Joseph and Pharaoh

After giving Pharaoh the understanding of the dreams, Joseph also gave a word of wisdom:

> *"Now therefore, let Pharaoh select a discerning and wise man, and set him over the land of Egypt. Let Pharaoh do this, and let him appoint officers over the land, to collect one-fifth of the produce of the land of Egypt in the seven plentiful years. And let them gather all the food of those good years that are coming, and store up grain under the authority of Pharaoh, and let them keep food in the cities. Then that food shall be as a reserve for the land for the seven years of famine which shall be in the land of Egypt, that the land may not perish during the famine" (Genesis 41: 33-36).*

Pharaoh responded by appointing Joseph to implement this measure. As a result, the position of Egypt was strengthened and, during the seven years of famine, their stored grain resources were used to save not only their people but also other nations.

It's interesting to note, that none of the wise men and magicians of Egypt could interpret the dreams.

We see a different response when Joseph, as a young man, shares his own dreams to his Hebraic family.

> *Now Israel loved Joseph more than all his children, because he was the son of his old age. Also he made him a tunic of many colours. But when his brothers saw that their father loved him more than all his brothers, they hated him and could not speak peaceably to him.*
>
> *Now Joseph had a dream, and he told it to his brothers; and they hated him even more. So he said to them, "Please hear this dream which I have dreamed: There we were, binding sheaves in the field. Then behold, my sheaf arose and also stood upright; and indeed your sheaves stood all around and bowed down to my sheaf."*
>
> *And his brothers said to him, "Shall you indeed reign over us? Or shall you indeed have dominion over us?" So they hated him even more for his dreams and for his words.*
>
> *Then he dreamed still another dream and told it to his brothers, and said, "Look, I have dreamed another dream. And this time, the sun, the moon, and the eleven stars bowed down to me."*
>
> *So he told it to his father and his brothers; and his father rebuked him and said to him, "What is this dream that you have dreamed? Shall your mother and I and your brothers indeed come to bow down to the earth*

before you?" And his brothers envied him, but his father kept the matter in mind (Genesis 37:3-11).

We see from this account that the family of Joseph immediately understood the dreams and what they spoke of both for his future and the future of his family. We also see that the dreams were significant enough for Joseph's father (Israel) to continue to reflect on the dreams.

Although it took years to come to pass, we also see the fulfillment of these dreams when Pharaoh appointed Joseph as overseer of the collection of grain. Pharaoh was the only leader who out-ranked him. Eventually, Joseph's family came to Egypt where they literally bowed before the man who had become second to the most powerful leader in the known world.

Nebuchadnezzar and Daniel

Let's consider another Hebrew man, who interpreted dreams for a leader of another culture and another land. This is the story of Daniel, who interpreted Nebuchadnezzar's dreams. Daniel was a Hebrew captive who had risen to a place of influence with the ruler of the land.

I, Nebuchadnezzar, was at rest in my house, and flourishing in my palace. I saw a dream, which made me afraid, and the thoughts on my bed and the visions of my head troubled me. Therefore I issued a decree to bring in all the wise men of Babylon before me, that they might make known to me the interpretation of the dream. Then the magicians, the astrologers, the Chaldeans, and the soothsayers came in, and I told them the dream; but they did not make known to me its interpretation. But at last Daniel came before me (his name is Belteshazzar, according to the name of my god; in him is the Spirit of the Holy God), and I told the dream before him, saying: "Belteshazzar, chief of the magicians, because I know that the Spirit of the Holy God is in you, and no secret troubles you, explain to me the visions of my dream that I have seen, and its interpretation.

"These were the visions of my head while on my bed:

"I was looking, and behold, a tree in the midst of the earth, and its height was great. The tree grew and became strong; its height reached to the heavens, and it could be seen to the ends of all the earth. Its leaves were lovely, its fruit abundant, and in it was food for all. The beasts of the field found shade under it, the birds of the heavens dwelt in its branches, and all flesh was fed from it.

"I saw in the visions of my head while on my bed, and there was a

watcher, a holy one, coming down from heaven. He cried aloud and said thus:

'Chop down the tree and cut off its branches, strip off its leaves and scatter its fruit. Let the beasts get out from under it, and the birds from its branches. Nevertheless leave the stump and roots in the earth,

'Bound with a band of iron and bronze, in the tender grass of the field. Let it be wet with the dew of heaven, and let him graze with the beasts on the grass of the earth. Let his heart be changed from that of a man, let him be given the heart of a beast, and let seven times pass over him.

'This decision is by the decree of the watchers, and the sentence by the word of the holy ones, in order that the living may know that the Most High rules in the kingdom of men, gives it to whomever He will, and sets over it the lowest of men.'

'This dream I, King Nebuchadnezzar, have seen. Now you, Belteshazzar, declare its interpretation, since all the wise men of my kingdom are not able to make known to me the interpretation; but you are able, for the Spirit of the Holy God is in you.'"

Then Daniel, whose name was Belteshazzar, was astonished for a time, and his thoughts troubled him. So the king spoke, and said, "Belteshazzar, do not let the dream or its interpretation trouble you." Belteshazzar answered and said, "My lord, may the dream concern those who hate you, and its interpretation concern your enemies!

"The tree that you saw, which grew and became strong, whose height reached to the heavens and which could be seen by all the earth, whose leaves were lovely and its fruit abundant, in which was food for all, under which the beasts of the field dwelt, and in whose branches the birds of the heaven had their home— it is you, O king, who have grown and become strong; for your greatness has grown and reaches to the heavens, and your dominion to the end of the earth.

"And inasmuch as the king saw a watcher, a holy one, coming down from heaven and saying, 'Chop down the tree and destroy it, but leave its stump and roots in the earth, bound with a band of iron and bronze in the tender grass of the field; let it be wet with the dew of heaven, and let him graze with the beasts of the field, till seven times pass over him'; this is the interpretation, O king, and this is the decree of the Most High, which has come upon my lord the king: They shall drive you from men, your dwelling shall be with the beasts of the field, and they shall make

you eat grass like oxen. They shall wet you with the dew of heaven, and seven times shall pass over you, till you know that the Most High rules in the kingdom of men, and gives it to whomever He chooses.

"And inasmuch as they gave the command to leave the stump and roots of the tree, your kingdom shall be assured to you, after you come to know that Heaven rules. Therefore, O king, let my advice be acceptable to you; break off your sins by being righteous, and your iniquities by showing mercy to the poor. Perhaps there may be a lengthening of your prosperity" (Daniel 4:4-27).

Nebuchadnezzar had this dream and invited all the magicians and wise men to interpret it. None could. Daniel immediately understood the meaning of the dream. He also understood the link between the dream and the character and activities of Nebuchadnezzar.

Figure 2: Nebuchadnezzar and Daniel

Daniel knew that God spoke in dreams to show where changes need to be made in our character. God resists the proud but gives grace to the humble. God was showing Nebuchadnezzar what was about to happen in his life and why.

The fulfillment of the dream:

All this came upon King Nebuchadnezzar. At the end of the twelve months he was walking about the royal palace of Babylon. The king spoke, saying, "Is not this great Babylon, that I have built for a royal dwelling by my mighty power and for the honour of my majesty?"

While the word was still in the king's mouth, a voice fell from heaven: "King Nebuchadnezzar, to you it is spoken: the kingdom has departed from you! And they shall drive you from men, and your dwelling shall be with the beasts of the field. They shall make you eat grass like oxen; and seven times shall pass over you, until you know that the Most High rules in the kingdom of men, and gives it to whomever He chooses."

That very hour the word was fulfilled concerning Nebuchadnezzar; he was driven from men and ate grass like oxen; his body was wet with the dew of heaven till his hair had grown like eagles' feathers and his nails like birds' claws.

And at the end of the time, I, Nebuchadnezzar, lifted my eyes to heaven, and my understanding returned to me; and I blessed the Most High and praised and honoured Him who lives forever: "For His dominion is an everlasting dominion, and His kingdom is from generation to generation. All the inhabitants of the earth are reputed as nothing; He does according to His will in the army of heaven and among the inhabitants of the earth. No one can restrain His hand or say to Him, 'What have You done?'"

At the same time, my reason returned to me, and for the glory of my kingdom, my honour and splendour returned to me. My counsellors and nobles resorted to me, I was restored to my kingdom, and excellent majesty was added to me. Now I, Nebuchadnezzar, praise and extol and honour the King of heaven, all of whose works are truth, and His ways justice. And those who walk in pride He is able to put down (Daniel 4: 28-37).

This was another account where a Hebrew understood the meaning of a dream but the people of the foreign culture didn't understand. The

Hebrew people knew that God spoke in dreams and that He used the symbols of dreams to communicate the message.

DREAMS AND VISIONS FROM THE NEW TESTAMENT

Dreams and visions are not limited to the Old Testament, but are prominent in the New Testament as well.

Joseph had a dream about marrying Mary even though she was pregnant:

> *But while he thought about these things, behold, an angel of the Lord appeared to him in a dream, saying, "Joseph, son of David, do not be afraid to take to you Mary your wife, for that which is conceived in her is of the Holy Spirit (Matthew 1:20).*

The wise men from the east were warned in a dream that they should not return to Herod after finding the child they were seeking:

> *Then, being divinely warned in a dream that they should not return to Herod, they departed for their own country another way (Matthew 2:12).*

Joseph had a dream to escape with the mother and child to Egypt to protect him from Herod:

> *Now when they had departed, behold, an angel of the Lord appeared to Joseph in a dream, saying, "Arise, take the young Child and His mother, flee to Egypt, and stay there until I bring you word; for Herod will seek the young Child to destroy Him" (Matthew 2:13).*

Joseph dreamed that it was safe to return to Israel, with further wisdom leading him to go to Nazareth:

> *Now when Herod was dead, behold, an angel of the Lord appeared in a dream to Joseph in Egypt, saying, "Arise, take the young Child and His mother, and go to the land of Israel, for those who sought the young Child's life are dead." Then he arose, took the young Child and His mother, and came into the land of Israel.*

> *But when he heard that Archelaus was reigning over Judea instead of his father Herod, he was afraid to go there. And being warned by God in a dream, he turned aside into the region of Galilee. And he came and dwelt in a city called Nazareth, that it might be fulfilled which was spoken by the prophets, "He shall be called a Nazarene" (Matthew 2:*

19-23).

Pilate's wife dreamed of the righteousness of Jesus, and warned her husband:

> *While he was sitting on the judgment seat, his wife sent to him, saying, "Have nothing to do with that just Man, for I have suffered many things today in a dream because of Him" (Matthew 27:19).*

Zacharias had a vision in the temple:

> *Then an angel of the Lord appeared to him, standing on the right side of the altar of incense (Luke 1:11).*

Ananias had a vision to go and pray for Saul's healing:

> *So the Lord said to him, "Arise and go to the street called Straight, and inquire at the house of Judas for one called Saul of Tarsus, for behold, he is praying (Acts 9:11).*

Cornelius (a gentile or non-Jew but one who "prayed to God always") had a vision to send for Peter to tell him what to do:

> *About the ninth hour of the day he saw clearly in a vision an angel of God coming in and saying to him, "Cornelius!"*

> *And when he observed him, he was afraid, and said, "What is it, lord?"*

> *So he said to him, "Your prayers and your alms have come up for a memorial before God. Now send men to Joppa, and send for Simon whose surname is Peter. He is lodging with Simon, a tanner, whose house is by the sea. He will tell you what you must do" (Acts 10:3-6).*

Peter had a vision of being told to eat non-kosher food and not to call unclean what God had cleansed (symbolic of Cornelius the non-Jew whom God was sending Peter to see):

> *The next day, as they went on their journey and drew near the city, Peter went up on the housetop to pray, about the sixth hour. Then he became very hungry and wanted to eat; but while they made ready, he fell into a trance and saw heaven opened and an object like a great sheet bound at the four corners, descending to him and let down to the earth. In it were all kinds of four-footed animals of the earth, wild beasts, creeping things, and birds of the air. And a voice came to him, "Rise, Peter; kill and*

eat."

But Peter said, "Not so, Lord! For I have never eaten anything common or unclean."

And a voice spoke to him again the second time, "What God has cleansed you must not call common." This was done three times. And the object was taken up into heaven again (Acts 10:9-16).

Paul had a vision of the need to go to Macedonia:

And a vision appeared to Paul in the night. A man of Macedonia stood and pleaded with him, saying, "Come over to Macedonia and help us" (Acts 16:9).

There are many other visions and dreams in the Bible including entire books that are accounts of visions. Clearly, as reflected in the Bible, God intends the interpretation of dreams and visions as a key factor in the relationship between God and those who seek Him.

MODERN-DAY VISIONS AND DREAMS

Otto Loewi (1873-1961), a German physiologist, won the Nobel Prize for medicine in 1936 for his work on the chemical transmission of nerve impulses. In 1903, Loewi had the idea that there might be a chemical transmission of the nervous impulse rather than an electrical one, which was the understanding of that time, but he did not know how to prove this. He didn't know how to pursue his idea and no longer focused on that until 17 years later when he dreamed the following:

"The night before Easter Sunday of that year I awoke, turned on the light, and jotted down a few notes on a tiny slip of paper. Then I fell asleep again. It occurred to me at 6 o'clock in the morning that during the night I had written down something most important, but I was unable to decipher the scrawl. The next night, at 3 o'clock, the idea returned. It was the design of an experiment to determine whether or not the hypothesis of chemical transmission that I had uttered 17 years ago was correct. I got up immediately, went to the laboratory, and performed a single experiment on a frog's heart according to the nocturnal design."

It took Loewi ten years to establish his idea through a series of tests. Ultimately the result of his initial dream-induced experiment became the basis for the theory of chemical transmission of the nervous impulse. This led to a Nobel Prize for medicine.

Madame C.J. Sarah Breedlove Walker (1867-1919) was the first female American self-made millionaire. She was also the first member of her family born, not as a slave, but as a free person.

Madame Walker, (her business name), founded and built a highly successful African-American cosmetic company that made her a millionaire many times over. She suffered from a scalp infection that caused her to lose most of her hair. She experimented with patented medicines and hair-care products. Then she dreamed the solution:

As she put it "He answered my prayer, for one night I had a dream, and in that dream a big, black man appeared to me and told me what to mix up in my hair. Some of the remedy was grown in Africa, but I sent for it, mixed it, put it on my scalp, and in a few weeks my hair was coming in faster than it had ever fallen out. I tried it on my friends; it helped them. I made up my mind to begin to sell it."

Walker was an entrepreneur, philanthropist and social activist. She summed up her rise from a childhood in poverty to becoming the head of an international, multi-million dollar corporation with the following:

> *"I am a woman who came from the cotton fields of the South. From there I was promoted to the washtub. From there I was promoted to the cook kitchen. And from there I promoted myself into the business of manufacturing hair goods and preparations....I have built my own factory on my own ground."*

Albert Einstein (1879 – 1955) conceived the theory of relativity in a dream. He dreamed he was sledding down a steep mountain, going faster and faster, approaching the speed of light, which caused the stars in his dream to change their appearance. Meditating upon that dream, Einstein eventually worked out his extraordinary scientific achievement, the principle of relativity.

Frederick Banting (1891 – 1941) had two dreams that were the inspiration for experiments leading to the discovery of insulin. Insulin was eventually developed as a treatment for what would have been a fatal disease: type 1 Diabetes. Frederik Banting and Charles Best developed the treatment in 1921.

The Nobel prize-winning idea of how to treat diabetes with insulin came to Banting in a dream one night. With the help of Charles Best, he finally isolated the compound that has changed the lives of millions of diabetics ever since.

George Frideric Handel (1685-1759) is said to have received the last portion of "Messiah" in a dream.

Through the experience of these modern day people, we see that God uses dreams to give wisdom and speak to us of many things. He is speaking all the time but are we listening, understanding and remembering our dreams?

God speaks in our dreams about our destiny and purpose in life. He did this with Joseph and, since He doesn't have favourites, He will do this in your dreams.

If you have not been one to remember your dreams, before you go to sleep, ask Him to help you to remember and to help you understand what He is saying. Keep a pad of paper and pen by your bed and write down your dreams as soon as you wake. If you recall two or three dreams in one night, they usually are talking about the same thing although they may be from different perspectives.

Often, we will have a series of dreams that are all about the same theme over weeks or even months. You will begin to understand your dreams better as you ask God to help you understand and as you review and reflect on them.

Also, it's worth remembering that dreams are usually full of symbols so try to look at the dream as a parable. It may be easier for you to do this with a friend's dream before your own. This is usually because we are not so emotionally tied to the characters in someone else's dreams. In this way, we can more easily step back and see the big picture in the symbols.

With practice, you will understand your dreams more quickly as well.

Visions are often more literal so they may be taken more at face value. Young believers will often have visions or dreams that are more literal or sometimes part literal and part symbolic.

The longer we walk in relationship with God, the more symbolic and complex our dreams will be, requiring reflection, research and prayer to understand what God is saying.

Sometimes, we understand some of a dream, but have questions. We can ask the Holy Spirit to give us another dream in order to help us understand.

Remember that God is speaking from His heart as Father wanting you, the dreamer to receive His love and walk closer in relationship with Him. He loves everyone like a Father loves His children. He wants the dreamer to know how much they are loved.

References

"Inventions That Came in Dreams — Largest Compilation on the Internet." Dream Interpretation: Everything about Dreams, Man from Modesto, 26 Dec. 2010, dreamtraining.blogspot.com/2010/12/inventions-that-came-in-dreams-largest.html

3 PROTOCOLS WHEN GIVING INTERPRETATIONS

We have developed a protocol or set of guidelines to support the communication of interpretations to dreams or visions. The basis for the protocol is drawn from the following scripture:

THE LOVE CHAPTER

Though I speak with the tongues of men and of angels, but have not love, I have become sounding brass or a clanging cymbal. And though I have the gift of prophecy, and understand all mysteries and all knowledge, and though I have all faith, so that I could remove mountains, but have not love, I am nothing. And though I bestow all my goods to feed the poor, and though I give my body to be burned, but have not love, it profits me nothing.

Love suffers long and is kind; love does not envy; love does not parade itself, is not puffed up; does not behave rudely, does not seek its own, is not provoked, thinks no evil; does not rejoice in iniquity, but rejoices in the truth; bears all things, believes all things, hopes all things, endures all things.

Love never fails. But whether there are prophecies, they will fail; whether there are tongues, they will cease; whether there is knowledge, it will vanish away. For we know in part and we prophesy in part. But when that which is perfect has come, then that which is in part will be done away.

When I was a child, I spoke as a child, I understood as a child, I thought as a child; but when I became a man, I put away childish things. For now we see in a mirror, dimly, but then face to face. Now I know in part, but then I shall know just as I also am known.

And now abide faith, hope, love, these three; but the greatest of these is love (1 Corinthians 13).

ALWAYS SPEAK IN LOVE

In that love is our basic guideline, we filter interpretations through love and endeavour to keep to this protocol:

- Avoid adding anything to an interpretation, including any of the following:

    a. Teaching

    b. Counselling

    c. Disapproval

    d. Advice

    e. Direction

- Filter interpretations through love, and be merciful;

- Avoid using words with negative connotation;

- Avoid personal opinions; and

- Keep the dream and interpretation confidential (except with permission from the dreamer).

These basic guidelines are the same as those for giving prophetic words. We note this direction in the following scripture:

But he who prophesies speaks edification and exhortation and comfort to men (1 Corinthians 14:3).

Or to put that in a more modern vernacular:

The person who prophesies speaks to lift up, build up, and cheer up others.

We use this guideline to ensure that the interpretation of a dream or vision is given with a heart of love that draws inspiration from the Holy Spirit.

CONSIDER YOUR AUDIENCE

When one receives a request to interpret a dream from someone who has a limited understanding of God, or where the spiritual background of the dreamer is unknown, use only universally understood terminology and language. Avoid using all jargon.

For example, someone on the street speaks of having a dream where they are wearing a red jacket and helping people in a hospital setting. There is no other indication that the person has a spiritual background. One might respond to them that their dream shows they have a gift or strength for helping others who need healing.

TO SHARE OR NOT TO SHARE

For dreamers who dream about themselves and others; or dream about another person or group:

If the dreamer has contact with the group and a good relationship with them such that the group would be open to receiving the dream, the dreamer might consider passing the dream on to that group for prayer and discernment.

If the dreamer feels they know the meaning of the dream and are consulted concerning their understanding, it is appropriate to pass on what they believe to be the understanding of the dream.

If the dreamer has no contact with the group or feels the group may not be open to hearing from the dreamer, then the dreamer should pray in support of a positive message and for change of outcome if the message of the dream is negative. Many negative dreams are given for that purpose alone – prayer to change the circumstances.

Once you as the dreamer pass on the dream and, as appropriate, the interpretation, aside from prayer, your job is done. Where the response of the group appears to be indifference or even negative, it is important to accept that response and trust that you have done what God expects of you.

Character is more important than gifting. How we respond and manage our own response in these situations will determine whether we can be trusted by God to be used in future.

Even if the messages of dreams or interpretations are rejected, we must continue to hold our hearts open to God and to the people who may not be open to the messages. We need to be strong enough emotionally to trust God and maintain good relationships.

If we are wounded when messages are not received as we expect they should be, we risk isolating ourselves from others. The greater risk is that we may become emotionally stuck and waste time and emotional energy trying to get beyond the perceived rejection.

4 BEGINNING TO UNDERSTAND AND INTERPRET COMMON DREAMS

When we attempt to understand what God is saying to us in dreams, we pay attention to the pictures in the dream and what they mean to the dreamer. To understand what a symbol may mean, we use a number of different tools.

First, we look in the Bible to see if God is speaking to us using scripture or the same symbol as is used in the scripture.

For example, if you dream about crops, you might check an online Bible application that allows you to do a word search. You could simply key in the word 'crops' and the application would list all the verses where this word is found. You might then read these verses and reflect on them to see if you have a sense that God is speaking to you similarly as in one of these verses.

Sometimes, a symbol is not in scripture. In the case of a modern symbol, you could check a dictionary or an encyclopaedia. An example of a modern symbol in a dream is when we dream we are flying in an airplane or getting ready to fly at an airport. In these cases, we need to reflect on the modern understanding of these symbols and apply that to the dream.

God wants us to search out the understanding of the dream. It is how He is speaking to us. He wants us to reflect on the dream or vision and try to understand what He is saying. We can understand our own and other people's dreams and use this to open up people's understanding of what God is saying to them through their dreams.

COMMON DREAM IMAGES AND THEIR MEANING

Here are some common dream images and their understandings:

- **Teeth** that are loose or falling out usually means the dreamer is losing understanding or discernment.

    a. Losing eyeteeth may mean losing the ability to see important things in your life.

    b. Losing wisdom teeth may mean the dreamer is losing wisdom.

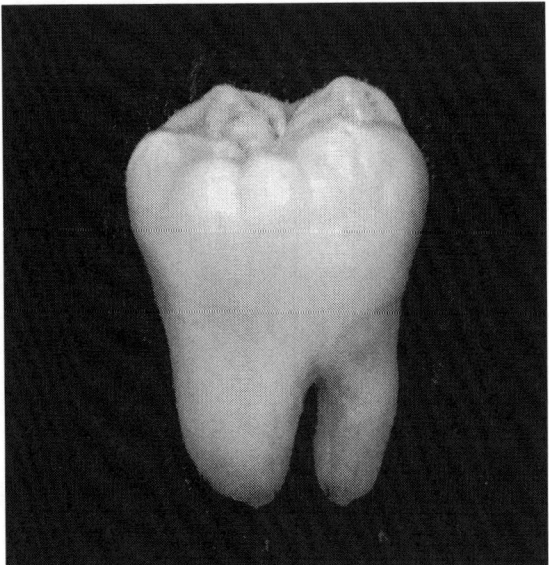

Figure 3: Dreams about teeth

- Dreaming of **falling** usually means the dreamer is feeling that some area of their life is out of control and there is fear associated with this lack of control.

- Dreaming of being **naked in public** usually means the dreamer is feeling vulnerable and/or transparent in some area of their life.

- Dreaming of **taking a test** usually means the dreamer is being tested for purpose of promotion.

- Dreaming of **being back in school** taking a test usually means something important wasn't learned in an earlier part of the dreamer's journey and is now being taught again.

- Dreaming of **being chased** usually means the enemy is trying to generate fear. But reflect on the context of the dream because the dreamer may be running from God.

- Dreaming of **snakes** usually means the dreamer is being harassed by lies or deceptions; if the snake bites the dreamer, the lie is painful and may have lingering effects. If the snake is a python or boa constrictor, the attack is trying to squeeze the life out of the dreamer.

- Dreaming of **spiders** usually means that something the dreamer is involved in is negatively affecting his or her life and spiritual destiny and they may feel trapped or spiritually poisoned by the venom of spoken words.

- Dreaming of **alligators** usually means someone with influence has begun an attack of gossip negatively affecting the dreamer.

- Dreaming of **someone dying** usually means an end of an era like a career or an issue is coming to an end.

- Dreaming of **losing your purse or wallet** usually means the dreamer has lost or is looking for his or her purpose, identity and/or favour.

- Dreaming of a **deceased relative**, often a grandmother or grandfather usually refers to generational issues or blessings, depending on the context.

- Dreaming of a **past relationship** or returning to that relationship like a former girlfriend or boyfriend usually means the dreamer is falling into old habits and ways of thinking.

- Dreaming of **one's house** usually is speaking about some issue in the dreamer's life. Note details and rooms:

    a. **Bedroom** speaks of intimacy in relationship.

    b. **Bathroom** speaks of getting rid of what is not needed in one's life and is pictured often as dreamer on the toilet; or God may speak through having a shower in the bathroom as washing away things and bringing cleanness; or dreaming of being on the toilet in public speaks of getting rid of what is not needed but in a situation where everyone is aware of the purifying process.

   c. **Living room** speaks to relationships with family and friends.

   d. **Kitchen** speaks of preparation of food to eat which could be symbolic of teaching; eating around a table could be speaking of being nurtured together, receiving teaching together.

   e. **Basement** speaks of foundational/basic issues.

   f. **Attic** speaks of things from the past if it's about things stored there or the roof may speak to covering for the dreamer's life.

- Dreaming of **vehicles** usually involves what the dreamer is doing or created to do as well as their purpose in life.

- Dreaming of **flying** sometimes may be speaking to the dreamer's capacity to move in the spirit realm and rise above problems.

- Dreaming of **horses** speaks of power and authority. The colour of the horses speaks to the nature of that power and authority.

- Dreaming of **dogs** is a picture of friends, loyalty, companionship and protection. If the dog is growling, it may mean a friend will turn on you.

- Dreaming of **storms** usually speaks to some powerful force that is coming. If the storm is light or bright, it refers to something God is bringing. If the storm is dark, it is speaking about negative or destructive forces from powers of darkness.

- Frequent **nightmares** are common with children. These are usually a tactic of the enemy to intimidate, generate fear, dull sensitivity, and result in rejection of spiritual things, particularly dreams.

HELPFUL TIPS

When you begin to try to understand a dream and reflect on its meaning, here are some helpful tips:

1. Write it down.

- Many dreamers will keep a pad of paper and pen next to their bed so that as soon as they wake, they can copy it out, even in summary, and then more fully later in the day.

- Give the dream a title or name.

- Draw out the dream. This helps you to see through the eyes of the dreamer and to focus on symbols rather than emotions.

2. Who is the dream about?

- The dreamer alone

- The dreamer and others

- Others (like dreamer is viewing a play or observing a scene through someone else's eyes)

Figure 4: The Setting of the Dream

3. What is the setting of the dream?

- Daytime

- Nighttime or evening

4. Are there any common themes in the dream?

5. What is the main idea?

6. Does the theme of the dream fall into one of the categories of the common dream images?

7. If you are interpreting someone else's dream, is more clarification needed? Go back to the dreamer and ask questions.

8. Are there any symbols that may be a pun or play on words?

9. What is the reason or purpose for the dream to the dreamer

- For prayer

- For warning

- Impartation

- Healing

- Overcoming strongholds

- Wisdom

- Gifts of spirit (word of knowledge, prophecy, etc.)

FOR THE DREAMER OR OTHERS?

Most dreams are about and for the dreamer. A smaller number are about others. A dream about ...

- the dreamer alone is for the dreamer;

- the dreamer and others is about the dreamer and that group;

- others only is not for the dreamer but likely given for the purpose of prayer and intercession.

COMMON DREAM SYMBOLS

Pay careful attention to common dream symbols:

Setting of the dream, such as if the dream is in ...

- colour or a daytime setting, the dream is a message from God;

- black and white or set at night or in the evening, it's about something the dreamer fears, or a warfare dream.

People – if the person is ...

- faceless and bright, it's an angel;

- faceless and dark, it represents a demonic force;

- known by name in the dream, find out the meaning of that name. That may be a key to understanding the dream.

Figure 5: Objects in dreams

Objects

- Knife or sword may be a weapon of war or a symbol of power and authority.

- Gun may be a symbol of power and accuracy

- Dart may be a symbol of curses or attack

Modes of Transport

- Bicycle may be one's individual ministry, calling or job but requiring effort to move forward

- Motorcycle may represent one's individual ministry, calling or job but moving forward with power

- Car may be one's ministry, calling or job but also possibly involving other people

- Bus may be the dreamer and others in an organization moving forward

- Train may represent a move of God

- Truck may represent a ministry, calling or job that carries resources to others

- Plane may represent flying high and overcoming as an organization if it seats many people or if it's a single seat, flying high as an individual

- Ship may represent the work or ministry of an organization in the world (sea is often symbolic of the world)

Clothing, such as if the clothing ...

- has a hole or is worn, something may need repair or may be worn out

- doesn't fit in the dream, possibly it means that the dreamer is walking in a wrong calling or the timing is off

- is swimwear or underwear, the dreamer may be feeling vulnerable in some situation

- is shorts, it may represent the dreamer's walk is able to be seen by others or they have a casual approach

- is another culture's clothing, the symbol may speak to a calling or intercession or short-term mission for what the clothing represents

- is a wedding dress, the symbol may speak to purity, covenant or readiness

- is shoes or lack of shoes, it may speak of the presence of or lack of peace or the gospel of good news

- is heels, may be symbolic of authority. If the dreamer's shoes have wooden heels, the authority is in the flesh

Creatures

- Snake usually means a deception or a long tale.

- Horse usually means a type of power and authority or it may mean a move of God.

- Cow usually means provision or a slow laborious change.

- Camel is usually symbolic of a burden bearer.

- Rat is a symbol of disease, it feeds on garbage.

- Spider is a symbol of the occult.

- Bees make honey and usually are symbolic of the glory of God.

- Hornet is symbolic of an unprovoked strike.

- Pig is symbolic of the demonic, something messy or unclean.

- Zebra is symbolic of some power that looks righteous but has soulish issues.

- Fish usually represents evangelism.

- Eagle is a picture of the prophetic.

- Owl is a symbol of prophetic intercession.

- Dog is a symbol of a friend, of loyalty, of a pet. Depending on the context of the dream, the loyal friend may be a symbolic picture of the Holy Spirit.

- Birds are often symbols of spirits; their colour will give you further understanding.

- Bat is symbolic of demonic torment, occult.

- Bear is a demonic force that is hungry for what you have or it may be symbolic of a hibernating issue.

- Cat may represent independent thinking or a familiar spirit.

- Donkey may represent stubbornness.

- Dragon is symbolic of Satan or his plans.

- Duck may represent a charlatan or 'quack.'

- Elephant may represent a big issue.

- Frog may represent a spirit of lust.

Weather

- Storms that are dark are from the enemy; if they are light, they are from God.

- Wind is a symbol of the Holy Spirit.

- Rain is a symbol of God's mercy, cleansing, outpouring of the Holy Spirit.

- Earthquake is symbolic of a great shaking or judgment.

- Fire is symbolic of a refining, or of God devouring the enemy.

Body Parts

- Thigh is a symbol for faith.

- Nose is a symbol for discernment.

- Neck may represent the will or willingness.

- Head may represent rank.

- Forehead is a symbol for thinking or the mind.

- Hair is often a symbol of wisdom and spiritual strength.

- Hand is a symbol for relationship or fellowship.

- Digits of the hand:

    a. Thumb may speak to the apostle, apostolic;

    b. Forefinger may speak to the prophet, prophetic;

    c. Middle finger may speak to the evangelist, evangelistic;

    d. Ring finger may speak to the pastor, pastoral, covenant;

    e. Pinkie finger may speak to teacher, teaching.

- Arm is a symbol of strength or power.

- Teeth are symbolic of the ability to understand.

- Blood is a symbol of life.

- Belly may be a symbol representing emotions or vulnerability.

- Breasts may be a symbol of nurturing or intimacy.

- Ears are symbolic of hearing and reception.

- Eyes are symbolic of the ability to see or have insight.

- Knees may be a symbol of prayer.

- Feet are symbolic of walking in the spirit, the peace of God, lowliness or humility.

- Left side is symbolic of something you were born with.

- Right side is symbolic of something God-given.

Colours

- Red is symbolic of wisdom or anointing or, depending on the context, may represent war, anger, or hatred.

- Pink may be symbolic of passion or emotion or in a negative context may represent the flesh.

- Orange is symbolic of perseverance and fruitfulness or in a negative context may represent stubbornness or rebellion.

- Gold is symbolic of God's glory or treasures or in a negative context may represent idolatry or greed.

- Yellow is symbolic of hope and light or in a negative context may represent cowardice or weakness.

- Green is symbolic of growth, prosperity, health, conscience, or a new beginning or in a negative context may represent pride, envy or the flesh.

Figure 6: Colours in dreams

- Dark blue is symbolic of spiritual communion with God, prophet, revelation, heaven or in a negative context it may represent depression, sorrow or anxiety.

- Cyan blue is symbolic of fasting and the human will or may speak to a strong will. Light blue may represent immature development of a person's spiritual gift, or the spirit of man or depending on the context it may speak to corruption or a demonic force.

- Purple is symbolic of authority, the apostle or apostolic, or intercession. In a negative context it can represent false authority or dishonesty.

- White is symbolic of the Spirit of the Lord, holy power or purity. In a negative context it may represent a religious spirit or witchcraft.

- Silver is symbolic of salvation or in a negative context may represent legalism or slavery.

- Black may represent formality or elegance or wealth or in a negative context may represent sin, grief, death, famine, or the demonic.

- Brown may be symbolic of compassion, pastoral, or humility or in a negative context may represent humanism.

Numbers

1 = God

2 = Division, judgement, multiplication, split

3 = Godhead, Trinity

4 = God's creative works

5 = Grace, redemption

6 = Man

7 = Complete, perfection

8 = New beginnings, teacher

9 = Evangelist, judgement

10 = Journey, pastor, wilderness

11 = Prophet, revelation, transition

12 = Apostle, government

13 = Rebellion

14 = Double anointing

15 = Mercy, pardon, reprieve

16 = Established beginnings

17 = Elections or elect

18 = Established blessing, established judgement

24	= Elders around the throne
30	= Begin ministry
40	= Completed rule, generation
50	= Freedom, jubilee
120	= End of flesh
153	= Kingdom multiplication
555	= Triple grace
666	= Full lawlessness
888	= Resurrection
1500	= Authority, light, power

5 EXAMPLES OF DREAMS AND THEIR INTERPRETATIONS

Following are some dreams along with their interpretation to help you as you begin your journey in understanding dreams. I begin with asking the same question you should ask when attempting to understand dreams — who is this dream about?

EXAMPLE A: HIGH FLYERS

Who is the dream about? The dreamer.

Dream:

I was with my family on the front lawn of my house and observing a plane quickly descending in the sky. Next I saw people floating toward me some were riding on individual sailboats in the wind, others were just coming toward me on the wind. There were both men and women dressed in business clothes, some of them carrying briefcases. I thought they must be coming from the plane that just went down. Next I saw the tree on our front lawn was bearing five different types of fruit. These were just falling off the tree into our laps.

Interpretation:

You the dreamer are being shown that in the future, after you witness the fall of a "high flying" group, many will quickly be drawn/brought to your home or group by a spiritual move. These men and women will bring the special ability to reach into the marketplace and bring the tools that are needed to accomplish it. Your leadership will experience much grace as the varied fruit seems to just "fall into your laps" without effort on your part.

EXAMPLE B: SAILOR SARAH

Who is the dream about? The dreamer.

Dream

I dreamed I was walking with a young girl dressed in a blue and white sailor suit. Her name was Sarah. I didn't recognize her as someone I knew in my life but I knew her in the dream. I believe I saw or wrote A to P or A - P and said her destiny from the beginning was to see and read (A - P?) the Christ. I walked with her through a university area or town and she was happy. People were attracted to her but I wanted to caution her not to allow herself to be distracted now.

Interpretation:

The dream suggests that you will be used to mentor and encourage a young ministry. This ministry has a destiny of walking in revelation and holy power. The dream shows that people will be attracted to this ministry and that you will have a part in teaching those in the ministry to stay focused.

EXAMPLE C: RESURRECTED GROCER

Who is the dream about? The dreamer and others.

Background information: In this dream, a young man was reminded of a church split 10 years previously when he felt rejected by the pastor and his family also felt rejected.

Dream:

In the dream, the dreamer's father had been the last customer of a local grocer a few moments before the grocer died of a heart attack. In the ten years that followed, the dreamer's father was rumoured to have caused the heart attack. At the end of ten years, the grocer, who was now resurrected, visited the family. Now, since this family was the first to be visited, there were rumours that the dreamer's father had something to do with the resurrection. The dreamer noticed and was disturbed by the grocer's hands which were missing multiple fingers from the time spent buried.

Interpretation:

This dream is for intercession. The dreamer is being shown that an old relationship that died years ago will be brought back to life. Yet it is also showing that within this relationship there is something missing, some ability to relate. It may have something to do with the hurts caused from the original issue.

EXAMPLE D: SO MANY BABIES

Who is the dream about? The dreamer and others.

Dream:

My husband and I were at a meeting of the prophets. Graham Cooke, one of the prophets, spoke to my husband and said that my husband's household would be like Graham's — his wife would be giving birth to a new baby every second day. Then we were given a baby — a baby from India. The baby was crying. We realized that we had to go home because we had work to do. We couldn't stay for the rest of the meeting. I was thinking, "Can I do it? So many babies and giving birth every second day?" While the baby was crying I said "Okay Jesus, this is your baby so you'll help us to raise this baby and all the babies."

Interpretation:

This is a dream for the dreamer and her husband. The Lord is telling you that He has a ministry and a destiny for you. When this begins it will be very fruitful and you may even have to change some of your plans. You will even question if you have the ability and resources to do this thing God has called you to. But you will also have the wisdom to know that even though it is your calling the ministry is the Lord's and He will sustain you and it.

EXAMPLE E: SOVIET METEOR SHOWER

Who is the dream about? Others.

Dream:

I was in a house inside what I thought was in 'soviet bloc' countries. I seemed to be a mother of two children — one boy between the age of five and seven and one girl around the age of two or three. I received a telephone call from my son's former girlfriend who said, "Just do me one favour and install Roman windows (or Roman blinds) in your new store." It was evening (dark outside) and the two children had gone outside to watch the evening sky. I noticed what was happening in the sky and went out to usher the children inside — it looked like a major meteor shower but the meteors were huge and made sounds like military weapons, missiles or something raining down. I knew this had happened once before. The boy turned to me and I could see that some kind of chemical reaction had occurred to his face and hand and they were 'eaten away' or dissolved. The last thing he said was "Why do you bite (or cut off) the hand that feeds you?" And I said as I took his arm with the dissolved hand "Because we love the hand that feeds us."

Interpretation:

This is a 'spying dream' given to show the plans of the enemy ahead of time. It was given prior to the Ukrainian Orange Revolution of 2004. I only fully understood this dream after praying into it for a number of months, and realized when events were occurring, the boy in the dream was Viktor Yushchenko and the girl was Yulia Tymoshenko. The mother represented the force behind the political interference of Russia. The dream was given for intercession for the destiny of the country of Ukraine and the people involved in the fight for its destiny. God was calling up prayer from His people to mitigate the plans of the enemy.

Initially, when I sent this dream to a respected international ministry for interpretation, they interpreted it but I felt their interpretation was not the understanding of it. Their interpretation did not ring true to me.

If the dreamer does not feel that an interpretation rings true to their spirit, then that interpretation is either incomplete or incorrect. In this case, I knew their interpretation was incorrect but I didn't yet understand it except I felt it had to do with Russia and the Ukraine since the Ukraine was known as the breadbasket of the former Soviet Union. So, I continued to pray.

Once the events of the Orange Revolution were occurring, I realized this was what the dream was about. I believe that even though there was a poison called Tetrachlorodibenzodioxin ingested by Yushchenko resulting in a disfigurement to his face, he survived the attack and was victorious in leading his country in a bloodless revolution to become a democratic nation with a duly elected leadership.

EXAMPLE F: THE SCOTTISH WOMAN

Who is the dream about? Others.

Dream:

I dreamt of my father's place with many family members there together, both those who had passed on and those still alive. I saw a Scottish woman speaking to a Middle Eastern Prince. She had discovered something in a diary of his and he led her to his own room where she would find out the key to this. It concerned an aspect of relationship with God that was not realized by most during periods of renewal or revival; but once realized, brings about a depth of oneness with God where signs and wonders are a normal daily outflow.

Interpretation:

This dream was given just prior to the Scottish Independence Referendum of 2014 and was for intercession for the destiny of Scotland, which was not a political separateness, but a oneness with the Lord that would result in an outflow of signs and wonders.

EXAMPLE G: A CHILD'S DREAM

Who is the dream about? The dreamer and others.

Dream:

Thanos, the bad guy with the gauntlet from the end of the Avengers movie, was attacking and wanted to steal the last stone for the gauntlet. The young boy dreamer was building a "rainbow" iron suit in the dream, but his rainbow lasers weren't powered up yet. Thanos attacks all the Avengers, and they seem defeated. Then Thanos was coming for him, but God came and powered up the suit with power crystals. The dreamer then shot rainbow lasers into Thanos' eyes. Then all the Avengers were fighting alongside him and they defeated Thanos together, so that he cannot complete his gauntlet.

Interpretation:

The dreamer is being built up and equipped by the promises of God. He will fight against the enemy alongside other heroes of faith, and God will give him the power to defeat the enemy with God's promises and protect against the destruction of infinity for humanity.

6 DEVELOPING YOUR DREAM LIFE AND INTERPRETATION SKILLS

Dreams and visions are the language of God. God speaks to us through them and wants us to figure out what He is saying.

Dreaming and seeing visions is associated with activity of the Holy Spirit in one's life. In order to develop in this area, we should seek more of the Holy Spirit in our lives.

Our dreams and visions are about God talking to us as His children and as we listen to what He says both in scripture and dreams and visions, we will grow in our character. God cares more about our character than any gifts He has given us. The vast majority of dreams that are about us are usually talking to us about our character and how God wants to help us grow. As long as we are responding to these dreams, God will keep giving us dreams.

When I was a young woman and first learning about the Holy Spirit, I was taught about the gift of tongues as one's personal prayer language, used to build one's faith.

He who speaks in a tongue edifies himself (1 Corinthians 14:4).

I was taught that using this gift, which is meant for all believers, is a key to building ones faith.

But you, beloved, building yourselves up on your most holy faith, praying in the Holy Spirit (Jude 20).

The phrase 'praying in/with the Holy Spirit' is used in Corinthians and contrasted with praying with the language of one's understanding to indicate or confirm that both should be used.

What is the conclusion then? I will pray with the spirit, and I will also pray with the understanding (1 Corinthians 14:15).

Paul said he thanked God he spoke in tongues more than all the believers:

I thank my God I speak with tongues more than you all (1 Corinthians 14:18).

If the apostle Paul thought this gift was so important that he felt compelled to point out that he used it more than all the Corinthian believers, its importance must be considered as vital to all believers.

When I was encouraged to use this gift as a young believer, I was given a goal of two hours a day. Some years later, I saw this same recommendation given by other teachers in the body of Christ.

I put this into practice in my life and found that this gift can be likened to the weights that an athlete uses to build muscle. The more repetitions and heavier the weights, the more capacity the athlete has to function in sport. I have found that as I regularly spent approximately two hours a day praying in the Spirit, as well as, reflecting on scripture, the more frequently and extensively I dreamed and received revelation. And the more I understood what God was saying.

I encourage you to consider the same recommendation; seek more of the Holy Spirit in your life. Spend time reading the scripture as a daily discipline and pray both in your natural language and in tongues for approximately two hours a day. Expect to see how enriched your dream life becomes.

The evidence for the use of the language of God to give hope and direction to His children is overwhelming. It is available and accessible to all. It is a precious but free gift from Him to express His love to men, women, and children throughout history. His desire is for us to use it!

Happy dreaming!

ABOUT THE AUTHOR

Carol Ann Henley and her husband David co-lead Lionsgate Community Fellowship, a ministry focused on partnering with the arts and entertainment community to reach out into the marketplace. Carol Ann has trained and provided leadership to prophetic evangelism teams during these outreach events. Carol Ann has taught on understanding dreams and visions locally, nationally and internationally over the past ten years. Carol Ann and David are ordained with Global Christian Ministry Forum.

Made in the USA
Monee, IL
17 May 2021